IMAGES
of America

ARKANSAS CITY
People, Places, and Events

In the late 1800s, Arkansas City began its sports tradition with baseball. Some of the early games were played at a baseball diamond east of town near the railroad tracks. Community members gathered for these displays of athleticism. From its inception, baseball became a popular means of entertainment. (Courtesy of Cherokee Strip Land Rush Museum.)

ON THE COVER: During the Great Depression, many of the movie theaters in town offered discounted shows for children. Huge assemblies of children on their bicycles often gathered to wait for movies at Starr Theater. Since the shows were an inexpensive means of entertainment, children looked forward to going to the movies. (Courtesy of Cherokee Strip Land Rush Museum.)

IMAGES
of America

ARKANSAS CITY
PEOPLE, PLACES, AND EVENTS

Heather D. Ferguson

ARCADIA
PUBLISHING

Copyright © 2011 by Heather D. Ferguson
ISBN 978-1-5316-3914-3

Published by Arcadia Publishing
Charleston, South Carolina

Library of Congress Control Number: 2010939906

For all general information, please contact Arcadia Publishing:
Telephone 843-853-2070
Fax 843-853-0044
E-mail sales@arcadiapublishing.com
For customer service and orders:
Toll-Free 1-888-313-2665

Visit us on the Internet at www.arcadiapublishing.com

Arkansas City: People, Places, and Events *is dedicated to my children, Hunter and Clayton, who inspire me every day. I love you both dearly.*

CONTENTS

Acknowledgments		6
Introduction		7
1.	Building a Town	9
2.	Business and Industry	21
3.	Entertainers	39
4.	Sports	47
5.	Clubs and Organizations	59
6.	Churches	71
7.	Law Enforcement	81
8.	Hospitals	95
9.	Schools	105
10.	Chilocco Indian Agricultural School	119

ACKNOWLEDGMENTS

In 2008, *Arkansas City, Kansas* was published. While researching and writing that book, there were many interesting stories that could not be included due to size constraints. It is believed that these stories should be told, hence *Arkansas City: People, Places, and Events*.

The Cherokee Strip Land Rush Museum's photograph collection has once again been utilized for this book. Unless otherwise noted, all images appear courtesy of the museum. What is not from that source has been gathered from people in the community, including Terry Eaton, Larry Rhodes, and Randy Walker. These wonderful individuals generously contributed images from their own collections in order to tell some of the stories that needed to be told. Thank you all for your contributions to the book and for your efforts to gather and interpret the history of Arkansas City.

Once again, Wilbur and Elaine Killblane have been instrumental in assisting with the research for this book. Wilbur has continued to contribute stories from the *Arkansas City Traveler* to our already extensive collection. He has also sought out information on topics that were needed to make this book complete. Thank you for your continued support and for your efforts to preserve the history of our community and to share it with others. I love you both!

Another special thank you goes out to my assistant, Jo Ann Bierle, for taking the time to read the material and point out proofing errors. Thank you, Jo!

Introduction

As demonstrated in the previous book about the town, Arkansas City has a rich history that is interesting on both local and national scales. The chronicle of the community parallels national stories and themes such as westward expansion, exploration, Prohibition, industrialization, and American Indian policy.

Arkansas City, Kansas, was founded in the 1870s in an effort to open up Native American lands for settlement. It was established by many great men and women who were seeking a new life. These people followed the call to move west and find an existence with fewer boundaries on land that was virtually free. The US government encouraged westward expansion, but in the pioneer mind it was God's will. They believed it their supreme right to spread their nation's boundaries, have the opportunity to improve themselves in regard to home and hearth, and often spread their church's word.

While many of the early people who settled the West became farmers and ranchers, some of them became industrious entrepreneurs starting new businesses that would become a part of a thriving community. Often, these men and women gave their all to create a new community that would be an ideal place for others to come to. Some of these individuals even contributed most of their own wealth that had been gathered through the creation of business and industry to bring people to town or to pay off community debts. In the end, they sometimes broke themselves for the betterment of the group.

The Walnut Town Company, sometimes referred to as the Creswell Town Company, settled Arkansas City in 1870 with a brilliant group of men setting their stakes on an area of land between the Walnut and Arkansas Rivers. Men such as G.H. Norton, Prof. H.B. Norton, A.A. Newman, H.P. Farrar, the McLaughlins, and several more were influential in the start of Arkansas City's businesses and industry. The founders of Arkansas City all held a stake in the town. Each and every one of them put some sort of risk forward in order to see the community succeed.

One
BUILDING A TOWN

Arkansas City, Kansas, was founded by men and women with a vision. The individuals who first arrived knew what they wanted their town to be and sought to create a vital, thriving community. They went out and recruited people who could fulfill the needs of the settlers. Many of the founders of Arkansas City started their own ventures, but if there was a need for a certain type of enterprise, they sought it out and brought it to town.

The founders often capitalized these businesses, and land was given to the merchants to locate their establishments. A.A. Newman, Capt. H.G. Norton, and Maj. William M. Sleeth were often the men who financed these concerns. Not only did these men bring business to town, but they also brought industry. Many of the early leaders lobbied to bring the railroad through Arkansas City, and it became a huge hub for five rail lines: the Atchison, Topeka and Santa Fe; the Frisco; the Midland Valley; the Missouri Pacific; and the Kansas Southwestern. Newman and a few others also built the power canal, which was used to supply energy to the many factories along its path.

By bringing in food, clothing, and jobs, the founders and early businessmen of Arkansas City supplied those who came to live here. Their general stores outfitted the town and the Indian Territory. When more people arrived, they generated more merchants with many items such as clothing, farm implements, food, and more. Additionally, the leading benefactors established farms and ranches around the community and invested in outlying communities. Newman was a major backer of Gueda Springs, which became a major location for healing mineral waters.

Early Arkansas City was the hub it was hoped to be. This trend lasted for many years. If something were needed, it was brought to town or someone started it on their own. The Protestant work ethic was alive and well in early Arkansas City.

W. M. SLEETH, President.   **H. P. FARRAR, Cashier.**

Cowley County Bank.

ARKANSAS CITY, KANSAS.

Does a General Banking Business.

Interest Allowed on Time Deposits.

——Domestic and Foreign Exchange Bought and Sold.——

COLLECTIONS PROMPTLY ATTENDED TO.

CORRESPONDENTS:

THIRD NATIONAL BANK, New York.
FIRST NATIONAL BANK, Kansas City, Mo.
WICHITA SAVINGS BANK, Wichita, Kansas

An often overlooked but very influential founder of Arkansas City was Maj. William M. Sleeth. Sleeth was born in Cambridge, Ohio. He was a Civil War veteran who went into the sawmill business in Fayetteville, Tennessee. In 1869, he traveled with the Nortons to Emporia, Kansas, and from there they progressed to what would become Arkansas City, stopping once in El Dorado on March 10, 1869. Sleeth opened the first sawmill in southern Kansas on the Walnut River, where Chestnut Avenue now crosses it. In 1870, Sleeth took a pawn of pistols and watches from the Gooch boys and Ben Cooper, who had just arrived in town, so they could purchase cottonwood lumber to build their claim shanties. All items were later redeemed. Sleeth ran his mill actively until 1873, when he helped start the Cowley County Bank. He ran what was then called the First National Bank until it failed in 1893. The bank failure debilitated him financially. He liquidated all of his assets and gave up everything he had to pay the depositors, all of whom received every last penny they had deposited in his bank. Sleeth went on to be involved in many other ventures, but the failure of the bank hurt him tremendously. He is a prime example of a founder of Arkansas City giving all that he had to help the town succeed.

Arkansas City was founded in January 1870. The town was platted in the spring of that year. John Harmon furnished the stakes for this venture.

Once the area was platted, people set out to build up a proper town. The first buildings included Norton's store, a hotel, various businesses, and cabins. The first hotel, the Woolsey Hotel, was completed and plastered by December 21, 1870.

Dr. Woolsey and his family came to Arkansas City in 1870. He constructed the Woolsey Hotel at 100 North Summit Street and built a stable nearby. His son Alfred and Billy Anderson purchased the stable in October 1874. (Courtesy of Larry Rhodes.)

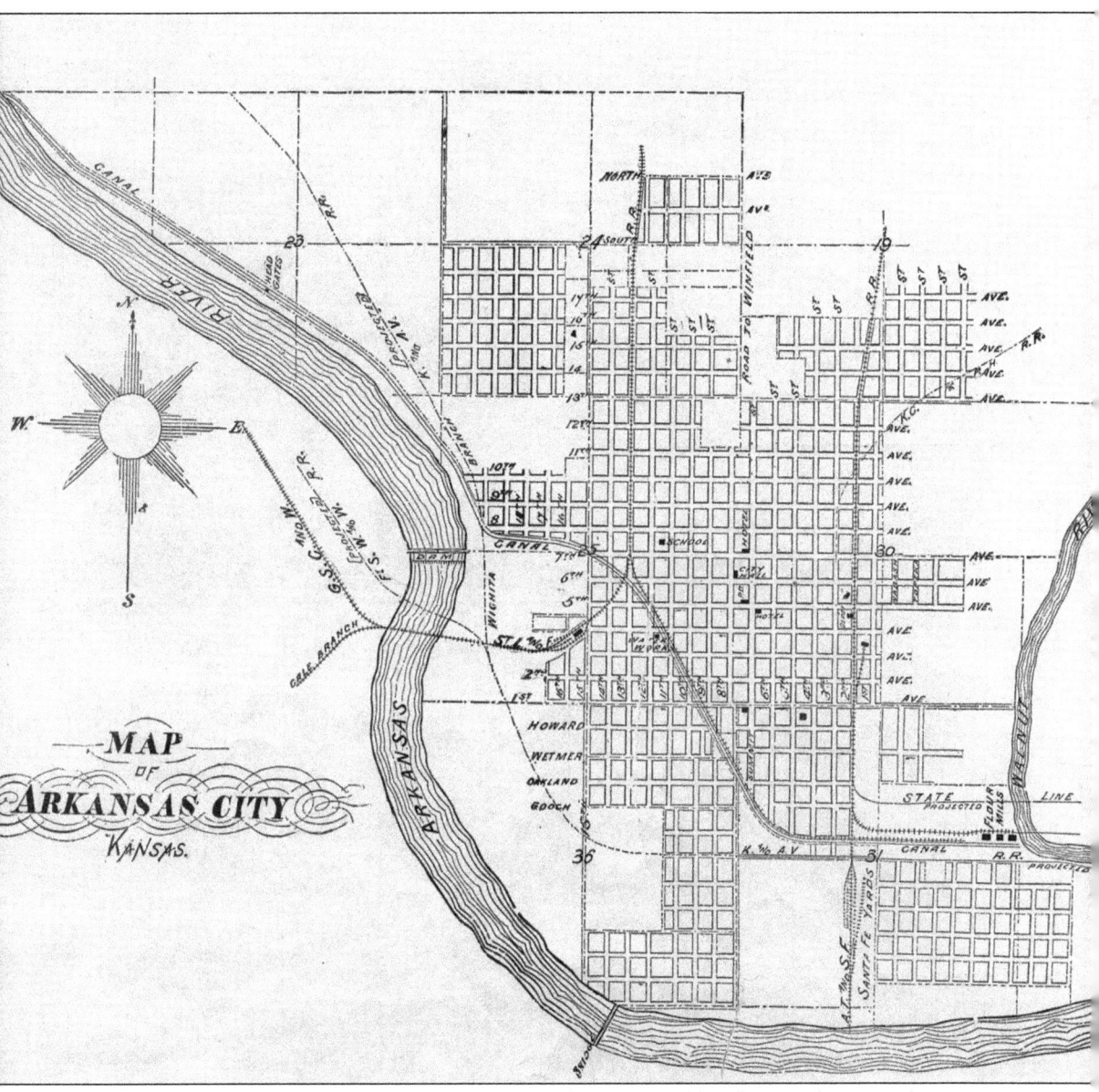

Cowley County was finally organized as such on February 28, 1871. The population at that time was a mere 550. H.C. Loomis was the first county clerk.

Sewell P. Channell was one of the first citizens in Arkansas City. He started a dry goods and grocery store in 1870, and his wife opened the first millinery shop the same year. Channell was the mayor in 1875 and 1876. In 1876, he served as a delegate representing the 89th district in the state convention. Channell wore many hats during his lifetime, including being a leader of the Masonic Lodge and the Knights of Honor.

The Walnut Bridge (pictured above and below in different years) was completed on May 28, 1871. The second bridge built in Arkansas City was the Sixth Street Bridge, which was a "company bridge," meaning that shares were sold in it. It was also a toll bridge, and the gatekeeper was "Peg-Leg" Davis, a Civil War veteran who had lost his leg, hence his name. The toll to cross the bridge was 50¢.

Post Office Building, Arkansas City, Kansas.

By 1872, the community finally had a post office. It was located inside the mercantile of Capt. H.G. Norton, who was the first postmaster. The second location, and first uptown, was at the corner of Summit Street and Central Avenue in the William Rowan Building. C.M. Scott was postmaster at the third post office site, at what would eventually become the Saddle Rock Café. The fourth location was on the 200 block of Summit Street (the west side), which was later Kuntz Clothing. Next, the post office was moved to West Fifth Avenue where the Fifth Avenue bookstore was later located. It then moved three times before arriving at its current location: first, three doors east on West Fifth Avenue to the Carder Building; second, to the Odd Fellows building on the corner of Fifth Avenue and First Street, where the first floor was specially built for the postal facility; and third, to Fifth Avenue and A Street, the location of today's public library. Eventually, the post office arrived at its current location—which has been its most permanent spot—at 220 South A Street. The postmasters from 1872 to 1922 were as follows: Capt. H.G. Norton, Aylmer D. Keith, C.M. Scott, Dr. Hughes, J.C. Topliff, M.N. Sinnott, W.H. Nelson, M.N. Sinnott, R.C. Howard, C.M. Scott, C.N. Hunt, and George Hartley. Mail was first carried by stage and then by the Atchison, Topeka and Santa Fe Railway.

Arkansas City had many early boosters. I.H. Bonsall had the first photography gallery from 1872 to 1884. Bonsall had been in the Army of the Ohio and the US Secret Service, and had gone on several missions for Gen. William Starke Rosecrans. Bonsall was the US Commissioner of Kansas for 10 years. He later became clerk of the city police, judge for the county, and then city commissioner.

THE FIRST HOUSE BUILT IN ARKANSAS CITY, IN THE SPRING OF 1870.—NOW THE PROPERTY OF JUDGE I. H. BONSALL.

Harry P. Farrar came to "Ark City" in 1872. He started his career here with the Farrar, Houghton and Shelburne Mercantile. Next, in 1875, he joined the banking business with his brother Fred and several other members of the community in the Cowley County Bank. His other involvements included Hill Investment, the A.C. Savings Building and Loan Association, Home National Bank, the Fifth Avenue Opera House, and many other business ventures.

J.H. Sherburne arrived in Arkansas City around 1873. He ran a general store and traded with the Ponca Indians in the 1880s. Sherburne became a rancher, was an active member of the Osage Livestock Association, and was a founder of the Main Cattle Company in 1884 along with N.C. Hinkley, S.P. Burress, H.P. Farrar, the Howard brothers, and Bradford Beall. The company was headquartered in Ark City, and the cattle were grazed on the Ponca Reservation.

James C. Topliff came to Arkansas City in 1872. He took a claim in Bolton Township, where he farmed for two years. In 1874, he moved to town and was a merchant until 1880 when he became the postmaster. Topliff was also a city council member in the 1880s.

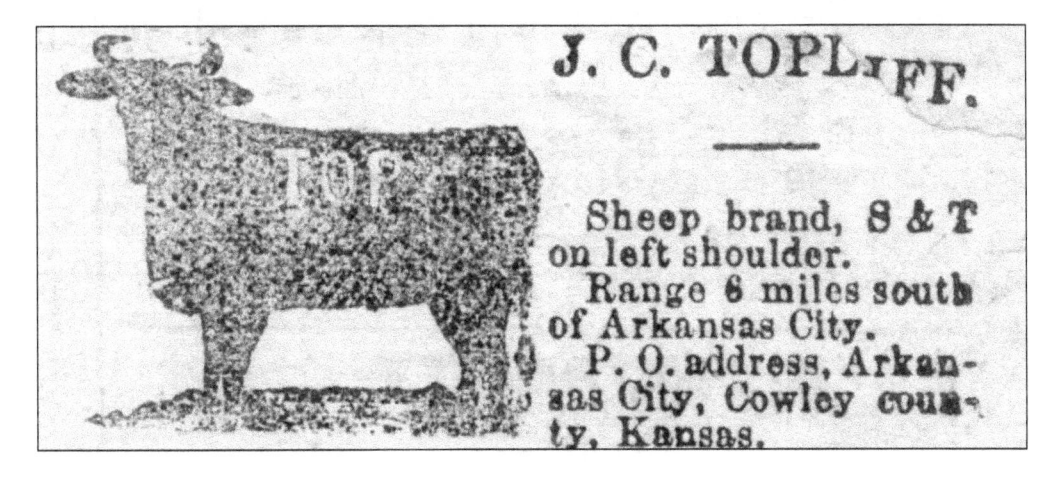

J. C. TOPLIFF.

Sheep brand, S & T on left shoulder.
Range 6 miles south of Arkansas City.
P. O. address, Arkansas City, Cowley county, Kansas.

Not all of early Arkansas City's famous characters were men. Lily Crampton moved to a farm southwest of Arkansas City when she was nine years old. She married E.C. Crampton on December 18, 1895. Being a farm girl, she became well versed in agriculture. She was in charge of the women's department in the Tri-County Fair and was a member of the Grange, a farmer's organization, for whom she lectured all over the country at conventions on behalf of Arkansas City.

Early Day Incidents and History of Growth are Related at Meeting of Grange Here.

Recently the Grange through arrangements made by Mr. and Mrs. E. C. Crampton, devoted a meeting to talks of early days in and about Arkansas City. On the occasion of the 54th anniversary of the city, The Traveler is publishing excerpts from the accounts which were reproduced by a stenographer furnished by the Chamber of Commerce.

Two

BUSINESS AND INDUSTRY

From the beginning, Arkansas City was a very industrial town (as mentioned in Images of America: *Arkansas City*). Like many communities from the 1870s through the turn of the century, Arkansas City wanted to be self-sustaining. The founders took great lengths to bring business and industry to the area. They had started a town, but they wanted it to be the best that it could be, so many invested in the community.

A.A. Newman, Major Sleeth, the Farrar family, and others put their money into the community by personally building resources that would bring industry to town and by taking out advertisements in area newspapers for the businesses that they would like to see come. They went so far as to stake new merchants. Such actions encouraged people to start their own businesses and made the city founders wealthy men.

These gentlemen also founded the Arkansas City Water-Power Company to power the many businesses that they would bring to town and those that were already here. Industries used the company's canal to power their factories, and manufacturers started businesses of all varieties. Arkansas City quickly became self-sufficient.

The merchants that were in Arkansas City took advantage of their closeness to the Indian Territory to make profits. They traveled to the Indian agencies to sell supplies and made contracts with the Army to supply military maneuvers at Camp Schofield in 1889. They supplied fresh beef and mutton, shoe polish, food supplies, and much more. Between 40 and 50 wagons came to Arkansas City per day for supplies. Workers from a local restaurant traveled to Chilocco Indian Agricultural School, which was directly across from the camp, and set up shop. The restaurant fed not only the officers but also the many citizens who traveled to the camp to watch or visit on a daily basis.

Early Ark Citians were entrepreneurs. They sought out opportunities and used them to make themselves rich. They supplied the community and much of Indian Territory with the goods that were needed to settle in an untamed land.

Arkansas City Planing Mill

FIRST STREET NEAR GLADSTONE HOTEL.

W. M. HENDERSON, Proprietor

Manufacturers of Jackson's Dry Cold Air Refrigerators, Doors, Sash, Stair Work, Mouldings, Turned and Scroll Work. A specialty made of circular work in door, windows and transoms, open or glased. Orders by mail wil receive prompt attention. Telephone No. 9.

In 1882, William Henderson opened a planing company one door south of Dank Brothers. He made sashes, doors, blinds, stairway railings, moldings, and more. Much of the decorative wood in the Fifth Avenue Hotel and American National Bank was made at his company. Henderson had a dry house capable of holding a full carload of lumber.

In 1884, Frank, Charles H., and John G. Dank moved to Arkansas City from Cincinnati, Ohio, and opened the Dank Bros. Machine Shop and Foundry. It was located one block west of the Gladstone Hotel. The foundry made the first steam engine in the area and performed every type of foundry work. (Courtesy of Larry Rhodes.)

Ranney's Fifth Avenue Hotel was almost completely built when Joseph Ranney came to town. He purchased it in 1889. The lodging was remodeled and reopened on April 20, 1905. R.K. Starkweather was the manager. In 1919, E.R. Ketner purchased the hotel. The property remained in operation for many years.

Duff & Oldroyd Furniture was opened in 1887 on the east side of Summit Street between Washington and Adams Avenues. The company sold wholesale and retail furniture and also provided undertakers. It sold furniture in southern Kansas, Indian Territory, and Oklahoma Territory. Duff & Oldroyd made parlor suites, folding beds, chamber sets, dining and center tables, armchairs, horned chairs, tricycles, and more.

The Empire Steam Laundry was opened in 1889 by Charles W. Hunt just to the north of the Gladstone Hotel. The laundry was state-of-the-art for the time. It had a Troy ironing machine that could iron 600 to 800 shirts per day, a Troy combined collar and cuff ironer that could handle 200 dozen cuffs and collars per day, a centrifugal steam wringer, and gas-heated irons. The lights and heat were gas-powered. (Above, courtesy of Larry Rhodes.)

Empire Steam Laundry.

A Growing Young Enterprise,

The Most Complete Laundry Between Wichita, Kansas, and Fort Worth, Texas.

THE HESS SADDLERY COMPANY.

A PROMINENT WHOLESALE AND RETAIL ESTABLISHMENT AND MANUFACTURER OF HARNESS AND SADDLES.

The Hess Saddlery Company was founded in 1893 by G.W. Hess. It was located at 104 Summit Street between Fifth and Central Avenues. Saddles, bridles, wagon covers, tent outfits, buggy tops, and more were made at the shop.

The Yost Yeast Factory was started in 1893. Jacob Yost was looking for a way to pay for the patent of his invention of a special chicken incubator and brooder. Well-known for the quality of her yeast, his wife suggested that they market it to make money. The first batches were sold from her kitchen, and eventually the Yosts built a factory to produce yeast at D and Poplar Streets. The factory made up to 5,000 boxes per month and sold the product under the brand name Sunflower. (Courtesy of Larry Rhodes.)

The Arkansas City Creamer began operations in 1899. It was located near the canal on West Madison Avenue, almost directly opposite of New Era Milling. The equipment was all top-of-the-line for the era, and the cream vat held 600 gallons of cream. Butter was produced at the plant by J.H. Knickerbocker. In 1902, the company was sold to J.P. Baden Produce Company of Winfield. (Courtesy of Larry Rhodes.)

In 1903, P.E. Henneberry and R.T. Keefe met while working at the John Morrell meat-processing plant in Ottumwa, Iowa. The two decided to start their own meatpacking business in Arkansas City, and construction on the plant began that same year. The name of the enterprise became Henneberry & Co.

Henneberry & Co. also constructed an ice plant that sold ice to farmers and to the A.C. Ice and Cold Storage Co. A.E. LeStourgeon operated the ice plant. In 1919, Henneberry's health began to fail, so Keefe became the manager. (Courtesy of Larry Rhodes.)

In 1920, the meatpacking plant became the Keefe-LeStourgeon plant. In 1929, however, LeStourgeon sold his stock to Keefe and then moved to Missouri. Keefe's children operated the plant until 1941, when A.B. Maurer and C.C. Neuer took over.

The Keefe-LeStourgeon plant then became known as Maurer-Neuer. On April 1, 1960, John Morrell and Company purchased the facility. It ran successfully until 1982 when it closed its doors for good. The plant had been a huge source of income for the community, and Arkansas City suffered from its loss.

In 1906, Arkansas City gained an ice cream factory. A.V. Franklin started his ice cream sales from home but soon decided he should open a manufacturing plant. It was operated with top-notch machinery. In May 1909, Franklin added butter to his line. By 1913, the factory was producing 500 gallons of ice cream a day and was selling product all over Kansas and Oklahoma. (Courtesy of Larry Rhodes.)

We Want You to Know That

Franklin's Sanitary ICE CREAM can be had at your Druggist or Confectioner's

Pasteurized Milk and Cream

Our Milk and Cream is Pateurized in all vessels, thoroughly sterilized. For the best in quality always use Franklin's.

Delivered to all Parts of City

Our Milk Wagon leaves for south part of city 8 a. m. For north part at 4 p. m. and south at 4 p.m.

For Prompt Delivery

Have your order by the above time. Our Ice Cream Wagon will deliver any time from 7 a. m. until 5 p. m.

Franklin Ice Cream Manufacturer
Phone 416

A. V. FRANKLIN, Prop.

In 1910, the Henry Roehl Company moved from Blackwell, Oklahoma, to Arkansas City. It was owned and operated by T.F. Henry and C.S. Roehl. The 20,000 Club, a version of today's chamber of commerce, brought them to town. The Henry Roehl Company made candy and ice cream, and was known for the Oh Henry! candy bar. The company was acquired by the Ranney Candy Company. (Courtesy of Larry Rhodes.)

The Waldschmidt Butts Motor Company was owned and operated by Sam Waldschmidt and Elmer Butts of Arkansas City. It was located at 610 South Summit Street. Waldschmidt built the two-story concrete building himself. The men repaired all kinds of vehicles, from cars to tractors, and in front of the building was a gas station. It was the first filling station with a repair shop behind it in town. (Both courtesy of Camille and David Pond.)

In 1919, the Arkansas City Hotel Association purchased the corner lot of Summit Street and Central Avenue from the Catholic church in order to build a hotel on the property. It was called the Osage Hotel. It was leased to John Sweet from Oklahoma City, Oklahoma, who opened it on November 3, 1920. Enlarged in 1924, it was known as "the best hotel in the country."

The Gladstone Hotel was opened in 1886 by Swan Sandstrum. It was a beautiful stone edifice located on the northwest corner of Summit Street and Seventh Avenue (now Chestnut Avenue). The basement housed a billiard hall, a barbershop, bathrooms, and a laundry room.

A dining room at the Gladstone Hotel was a favorite place for people to eat. The carpet for the upper floors was furnished by A.A. Newman and Co. The first floor was dedicated to office space, a reading room, kitchen, and carving rooms. On the second and third stories were 50 bedrooms, bathrooms, and toilet rooms.

After a couple of ownership changes, the Gladstone Hotel became a sanitarium in 1900. In 1922, the building was sold again, and in 1923, it became the Highland Hotel. The structure was resold in 1930 and became the Elmo Hotel.

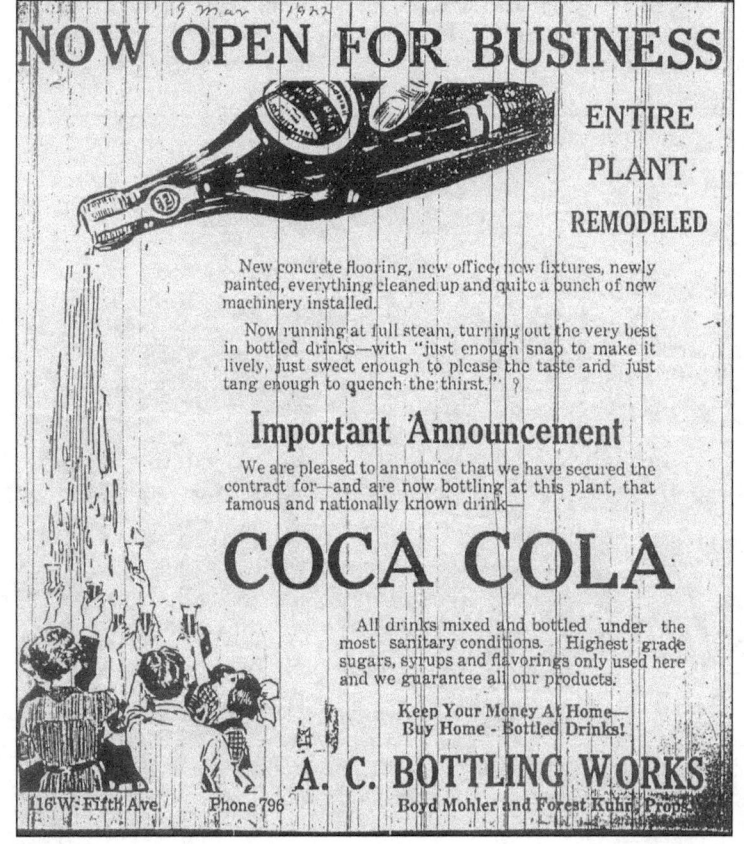

Arkansas City had several bottling companies. The A.C. Bottling Company was located at 1116 South Summit Street in the 1920s. Its main line of products included Coca-Cola, Orange Crush, and grape, cherry, lemon cream, strawberry, and lime sodas. Boyd Mohler and Forest Kuhn were the proprietors. (Above, courtesy of Larry Rhodes.)

The Dr. Pepper plant was first opened in Arkansas City on March 9, 1932. The plant produced Dr. Pepper, 7UP, and seven flavored sodas. The products were shipped all over Cowley and Sumner Counties in Kansas and Kay and Noble Counties in Oklahoma. (Courtesy of Larry Rhodes.)

The Kist Bottling Company was located 714 West Madison Avenue in the 1940s and 1950s. It produced many flavors of soda. (Courtesy of Larry Rhodes.)

Why Arkansas Citians And People In Surrounding Towns Ask For

Radley's VELVET Ice Cream

THE NATIONAL DISH!

BECAUSE IT
- is a body builder rich in vitamines,
- a balanced food containing all the elements of growth and repair.
- has a high percentage of tonic, invigorating mineral salts.
- is digestable and non-constipative.
- is the first food after operation, a standby in typhoid and a restorative to convalescents.
- tempts the appetite when other foods repel

KEEP IN MIND THAT VELVET ICE CREAM IS IDEAL
- with cereals at breakfast.
- as a busy man's between meal bite
- for dessert at all meals, alone or in combination with pies or fruits.
- as an afternoon invigorator.
- as a snack at bed-time.

ORDER VELVET ICE CREAM from your DEALER. VELVET ICE CREAM DEALERS always carry the largest variety of flavors and it is always fresh. Watch for our three layer BRICK and BULK specials each week.

RADLEY ICE CREAM COMPANY

316 West Madison Avenue   Phone 177

In 1924, the Radley Ice Cream Company, located at the corner of Sixth Street and Chestnut Avenue, was producing up to 750 gallons of ice cream per day. It offered a variety of flavors as well as Eskimo Pies. Business grew rapidly over the years due to the company's quality products. The plant supplied the town with many types of ice cream. By 1930, the company was purchased by Steffen Ice and Ice Cream Company. In 1927, Steffen's opened a milk products plant as well. More than 8,000 gallons of milk were brought in daily to the facility, which ran the product through separators and held it until it was ready to be made into powdered milk. The plant separated 12,600 pounds of milk per hour. The Steffen's plant grew over the years and expanded. However, in 1948, it was sold to the Arkansas City Cooperative Milk Association. (Below, courtesy of Larry Rhodes.)

Three
ENTERTAINERS

Arkansas City, Kansas, has had an incredible amount of very talented individuals born within its boundaries. The town has also been home to many famous entertainers at some point. It is almost unbelievable how many people from a town of 12,000 became well known for their abilities. There are very few communities the size of Arkansas City that can boast the same thing.

Arkansas City has had many musicians, singers, dancers, and such begin their careers here. The town has also had other, less-common versions of entertainment crop out of its population. There have been female bullfighters, jockeys, and much more. From the town's founding, its citizens worked at being cultured and learned in the arts. Early settlers brought musical instruments with them, and the first churches were quick to acquire organs and often held plays and musicals to entertain the community.

Music teachers, dance instructors, and the like taught their students at home or in studios around town. Often times, these students became the source for Arkansas City's entertainment. Many of them sang or danced at the Fifth Avenue Opera House, the Airdome, or other local theaters. Some performed in churches. One thing is certain: each contributed to Arkansas City before he or she went out into the world to make a fortune.

It is no wonder that with the earliest populations bringing instruments, the people who moved to Arkansas City would embrace music, theater, and other arts and make a mark on the world with their talents.

Nila Mac was born October 24, 1891, in Arkansas City. She was the only child of Margaret Bowen Mac and Don Carlos Mac. Nila started her road to stardom as a child, when she took dance from her mother at her studio. When the children put on recitals, they would be followed by public dances at Highland Hall, which is where the Burford Theater used to be, and at the Fifth Avenue Hotel. Nila was also fortunate enough to play the piano at the Airdome Theater as a child. The Airdome had drawn performers such as Fatty Arbuckle and Ozzie Nelson during its vaudeville days. In 1908, a year after her father's death, Nila's mother took her to New York City to take Chautauqua classes. Nila was recruited while in New York to travel with a touring theater group. She gave up touring after World War I, and she and her husband, Roy Briant, moved to Chicago. In Chicago, she ended up working for famous actress Alla Nazimova's theatrical company. Nila appeared in the 1916 movie *War Brides*, in which Nazimova starred.

Nila Mac's radio career began in 1929 when she went to work for CBS in New York. However, she was forced to leave CBS to return to Arkansas City to care for her sick mother. Mac took the job of director of a radio station while home. The radio station was located over the Fifth Avenue Hotel. After eight months at home, Mac was persuaded by CBS to return to New York to produce a children's show, *Let's Pretend*. The show took off and became renowned. She won more than 40 awards, including the 1943 Peabody Award for Outstanding Children's Program. The show was a success up until her death on January 20, 1953.

Harry Perico was born in 1882 and died in 1983. In between those years, he led an interesting life. He was born the son of White Horse, a warrior with Geronimo. He was sent to the Chilocco Indian School when he was 12 years old. Perico went on to graduate from college and teach journalism and English. He lived in Arkansas City for 50 years and during that time was involved in the Ark City Municipal Band, where he became known as "Mr. Trombone." (Courtesy of Terry Eaton.)

Edwin McCullum Druley was a very gifted musician. He was from Indiana but came to Arkansas City and made a splash. Druley taught many people how to play the piano, and he started an Arkansas City Music Teachers Association and a local Shakespeare club. His students were often given top ratings when applying at the college level.

E. M. DRULEY
Director of Orchestra

Well-known dancer Ernestine Day was born in Arkansas City in 1904. She began to learn dance at age 10 and told her parents as a young girl that she would be a dancer when she grew up. Day studied and traveled all over the world with the Denishawn Company of New York City in the 1920s and 1930s. She also performed at Carnegie Hall several times.

Max Lintecum was born in Fairfield, Iowa, on May 23, 1914. He came to Arkansas City as a child, grew up there, and was educated in the local schools. Lintecum later became an orchestra leader in Arkansas City and went on to arrange music for Clyde McCoy's Sugar Blues orchestra. He played in bands all over the country. He was killed in a car accident in March 1950.

BONNIE BROOKE

By 1917, Bonnie Brooke, of Arkansas City, had become renowned for singing folk music from around the world. She had educated herself in languages and cultures from many countries, including Germany, France, and others, and imparted her love for them through song.

43

Soloist Of Early-Day Shows Back To City After 36 Years

Kenneth Helwig, who was raised in Arkansas City, began his career as a soloist for silent film who provided vocal accompaniment for the illustrated songs shown during the movie. He worked in the film industry for more than 36 years. When he visited Arkansas City in 1948, he had worked several jobs from prop man for the American Film Company to property foreman for RKO Pictures in Hollywood.

Jess Meeker, son of Mr. and Mrs. H.W. Meeker and an Arkansas City native, accepted a position with the Denishawn Dancers in New York City at the age of 21. He started as an accompanist and moved up to composing symphonies for Ted Shawn and performing with the New York Philharmonic. When World War II broke out, Meeker did not leave the stage behind. Even as an artilleryman, he continued to perform for the men at Fort Meade, Maryland.

Murray Meeker, Jess's brother, was raised in Arkansas City. In 1939, he became the conductor and director of the Amarillo Symphony Orchestra in Texas. That same year, he was a guest conductor of the Louisville Symphony Orchestra and performed works by his brother, Jess, who played the piano.

Born in Arkansas City in 1919, William Guthrie was the son of Mr. and Mrs. F.F. Guthrie. He started music lessons at 11 years old. His teacher was Professor Druley, from whom he learned piano, harmony, and organ. In high school, William learned to play the coronet from Archie San Romani. William went on to teach at Westminster College of Music, where he directed the choir. In 1947, his choir performed with the New York Philharmonic. He later went on to teach at Carroll College in Waukesha, Wisconsin. Guthrie personally sang under the direction of John Finley Williamson, Arturo Toscanini, Sergei Rachmaninoff, and others.

Four

SPORTS

Arkansas City may be a smaller town than most, but it has a large amount of people who have made a career in athletics or have made a name for themselves on the field. Not only have there been superb athletes in recent years, but there were also great sportsmen in earlier times.

In 1898, Arkansas City's first football team was organized by local men who ordered the rules and playbooks and taught themselves the game. The only members who had actually even seen the game played were Ralph Dixon and Harry Hatch. The team practiced for a year and started playing teams in Fort Sill, Oklahoma; Carthage, Missouri; Wellington and Winfield, Kansas; Oklahoma City; the Chilocco Indian Agricultural School; and Oklahoma University. In 1898, this ragtag team won every competition. Another football team of note was the Tigers. This squad was also very competitive. The Tigers beat the University of Oklahoma Sooners and the El Reno Soldiers. Former members of the Tigers include Warren Gill, Jay Faircio, Benny Owen, Arthur St. Ledger Mosse, Ed Ewing, and Lute Jones.

In 1877, a group of people met at Pierson's Hall to discuss organizing a baseball association. Officers elected for this task were manager J.H. Sherburne; secretary and treasurer H.M. Bacon; and directors R.C. Haywood, A.W. Berkey, L.P. Woodyard, and Will Mowry. The group even organized two teams to set up a first game. By 1899, there were already a few baseball teams. One of them was the Arkansas City Grays. This was a semipro team that played many other semipro teams in the area, including those from Blackwell, Ponca City, Oklahoma City, Enid, and sometimes Winfield. Baseball enjoyed a large following at this time. The whole town practically shut down to watch the game. The Grays uniforms, with padded pants, were donated by New Era Milling Company.

Many early sportsmen have been entered into the Kansas Sports Hall of Fame. These individuals were great athletes who played for professional teams after college. There are several football players and baseball players in the Kansas State High School Activities Association Hall of Fame, and others are known for basketball, track, tennis, and coaching achievements.

From 1964 to 2003, Arkansas City had 18 wrestling state championships. The Ark City Takedown Club has had 91 champions in various weight classes from 1971 through 2010. In 1979, the Arkansas City High School football team won the state 5A championship. The school's baseball team won the 5A state championship in 2002. From 1995 to 2003, the high school girls' tennis team won five championships, and the boys' team had four championships from 1989 to 2007. Finally, the Arkansas City High School softball team had four championships from 1996 to 2007. That is a very impressive number of state champions from one small town.

Most of the individuals on the following pages are not known to Ark Citians, but they are known outside of town.

Arkansas City was once a center for horse races in the area. In April 1890, Arkansas City built a track where the breeders of the community could show off their excellent horse stock. At the track were stables where the horses were lodged. In 1900, the group of gentlemen who owned the track bandied the idea of a total remodel, but members decided it was more feasible to merely rebuild the fences. The area had become overgrown with grass, but after the rebuild, it again became an elegant track where horses could run once again. Racing matinees were held here for years.

Don't Miss The Races at Arkansas City, Saturday, October 24th.

DERBY DAY

Five Big Races Including The

Merchants' and Manufacturers' Derby

One Mile at Catch Weights.

Also a Free-for-all Pace and a Free-for-all Trot, a quarter mile pony race for boys and the funniest race you ever saw, a Mule Race of half a mile, any mule west of the Mississippi eligible to start. Gates open at 12 m., first race at 1 p. m. Admission 25 cents, Children 10 cents.

For privileges and other information apply to Gordon Parker, Sec'y., Ranney's Fifth Ave. Hotel, Arkansas City, Kansas.

Golf in Arkansas City began in 1916 when Mr. and Mrs. Earl Newman sank tomato cans into the northern hills two miles north of the city. The plan to make a country club was started by the Ark City Commercial Club. A committee was composed of R.T. Keefe, Foss Farrar, Bob Pollard, Ward Wright, Albert Newman, J.S. Younkin, Ralph Brows, William Stryker, and W.D. MacAllister. The present site east of town was chosen, and the club opened on December 14, 1916. (Both courtesy Larry Rhodes.)

CITY ASSURED OF MUNICIPAL GOLF COURSE

Over 300 Members are Already Signed Up; Elect Officers

The Municipal Golf Course was first laid out in 1923 The city decided to put in a course on the Vaughan, or Hess, tract located north of the aviation field and on the east side of the road. Membership was $12 per year. The city leased the land for $85 per year but purchased it in March 1925. This became Spring Hill Golf Course.

Arthur Kahler, better known as "Ox," played on the 1918 state championship basketball team for Arkansas City High School. He went on to earn 12 varsity letters at Southwestern College in Winfield, Kansas. He was an All-Kansas center in basketball three times and All-American twice. Kahler was a football, basketball, and track coach at Lyons and Coffeyville High Schools and a coach at both Sterling College in Sterling, Kansas, and Dickinson College in Carlisle, Pennsylvania. He was later the athletic director at his alma mater, Southwestern College. Kahler was inducted into the Kansas Sports Hall of Fame in 1974. (Both courtesy of the Kansas Sports Hall of Fame.)

Louis "Rabbit" Weller was not from Arkansas City, but he played football for both Haskell Institute and Chilocco Indian Agricultural School. In one game at Chilocco, he returned seven punts for touchdowns. In 1930, he was selected to the Knute Rockne All-American team and the United Press second team. Weller played two years of professional football for the Boston Redskins and the Tulsa Oilers. He was cited by *Ripley's Believe it or Not!* for returning a kickoff 105 yards for a touchdown. Weller was a charter inductee into the American Indian Athletic Hall of Fame and was inducted into the Kansas Sports Hall of Fame in 1977. (Both courtesy of the Kansas Sports Hall of Fame.)

In 1924, the Arkansas City Junior Chamber of Commerce started a half-mile car racetrack on West Chestnut Avenue. It was created to be a corporation, and shares were sold in the venture. Tickets to the races were to be 25¢ each. The actual track was not completed until 1927. In 1930, the American Automobile Association held a national-level race at the track on the Fourth of July. Races were held on the track for years.

In the 1930s, Howard Engleman was a star for the Arkansas City High School basketball team, which he led to a second-place finish in the 1936 Class A State Tournament. He later played for Dr. Phog Allen at the University of Kansas. He was the second player in the school's history to receive consensus All-American first team honors and helped Kansas win two Big Six Conference championships as well as a national championship in 1940. He was awarded many other accolades during his college career. Engleman played for the Phillips 66ers after college. (Both courtesy of the Kansas Sports Hall of Fame.)

Jack Mitchell was an all-around athlete at Arkansas City High School. He led the Ark Valley League in scoring in junior and senior high, was all-state in football as a senior, and almost won the state title in tennis. He was offered a scholarship by University of Kansas head coach Phog Allen. Mitchell attended the University of Texas in 1942 but went into the military during World War II. In 1946, he enrolled at the University of Oklahoma, where he was an All-American quarterback in 1948 and voted MVP of the 1949 Sugar Bowl. Mitchell was unable to go professional due to a shoulder injury, but following college he started coaching. First, he coached in a high school in Oklahoma, then he went to the college level at Tulsa, Texas Tech, Wichita State, Arkansas, and Kansas. He became a very well-known coach and had the pleasure of coaching Gale Sayers at Kansas. Mitchell was inducted into the Kansas Sports Hall of Fame in 2006. (Both courtesy of the Kansas Sports Hall of Fame.)

Sooner Greats

JACK MITCHELL
1946-1948

Arkansas City native Darren Daulton played many sports at Arkansas City High School, but he excelled in baseball. He was drafted in the 25th round in 1980 and went on to play 14 seasons with the Philadelphia Phillies and three with the Florida Marlins. While he was with the Phillies, they won the 1993 National League pennant. In 1997, his Marlins team won the World Series. Daulton then retired. He was inducted into the Kansas Sports Hall of Fame in 2006. (Both courtesy of the Kansas Sports Hall of Fame.)

Though Linda Hargrove is not originally from Arkansas City, she made a very large impact on the sports history of the community. Hargrove spent 17 years at Cowley County Community College as the women's basketball coach. She was named the NJCAA Coach of the Year in 1987. While at Cowley, she led the team to 10 league titles in 11 years. (Courtesy of the Kansas Sports Hall of Fame.)

At Wichita State University, Hargrove led the team to the school's first Missouri Valley Conference Championship in 1997. In 1993, she was named the conference's Coach of the Year, and in 1999, she was named head coach of the Portland Fire of the WNBA. She was named to the Kansas Sports Hall of Fame in 2007. (Courtesy of the Kansas Sports Hall of Fame.)

Five

CLUBS AND ORGANIZATIONS

Arkansas City's clubs and organizations began to form from the beginning as outlets of entertainment for citizens and as means for them to spend time around people with the same interests. For instance, associations sprang up for educational purposes, self-improvement, entertainment, and business connections.

In the 1880s and 1890s, groups formed to help veterans and their families. During Prohibition, a Women's Christian Temperance Union organized in town to promote abstinence from alcohol. Many civics clubs developed such as the Fortnightly Club, the Shakespeare Club, the Current History Club, the Avon Study Club, and the Chautauqua Reading Club. During each era of the town's settlement, different clubs were organized to address the current trends being set by the townsfolk. By 1929, Arkansas City had 175 women's clubs alone.

Throughout the history of the community, some unusual and intriguing groups have formed. A rather funny organization that was once among Arkansas City's Clubs was the Brotherhood of the Jangling Can. This brotherhood was formed in 1907 for those men who "have been canned" by their girls. Prospective members had to thoroughly convince the membership committee that they had been dropped by their girlfriends. Members had to sign a pledge that stated, "I hereby do solemnly swear that for the rest of my life I shall never show any preference for a woman unless she comes half way, and never shall indulge in love-making unless she does her share." Once in the club, the men in question received all of the sympathy that each man could offer another.

One very interesting club was the Izaak Walton League. The national organization was established in 1922, and a local chapter was formed in 1935. The league was dedicated to the belief in America's great outdoors. Gentlemen who belonged to this organization were very forward-thinking. They saved fish in dry spells, built feeders for quail, made turtle traps, stocked game fish in ponds, had crow shoots, and restored swampland. It is always a thought that the modern age is the only group that thinks about conservation of resources, but in 1935, Arkansas City men and others who belonged to the Izaak Walton League were steps ahead of modern society.

The Crescent Lodge of the Masons was formed on January 31, 1872, by Capt. O.C. Smith. Many of the prominent businessmen throughout Arkansas City history have been Masons. The Masons are a fraternal organization that donates to other nonprofits such as hospitals and schools. The lodge has moved several times. In 1921, it purchased the Fifth Avenue Opera House and operated from there. The lodge is still in existence today.

The Women's Relief of the Grand Army of the Republic (GAR) was formed in Arkansas City in 1885. The purpose of the organization was to "bring encouragement and cheer to the hearts of old soldiers of the G.A.R." Women who belonged to this organization donated to many projects such as relief from the 1923 flood, food baskets for soldiers and their families, and preparing rooms in hospitals for soldiers.

The local Independent Order of Odd Fellows, or IOOF, was organized on February 23, 1889, with 27 charter members and officers. In Arkansas City, the Canal City Lodge is lodge No. 352. It absorbed a previous local lodge, No. 160.

Rebekah-Odd Fellow Public Installation In IOOF Hall
3 Jan 1950

Arkansas City's Rebekah Lodge No. 88 was created in 1888. In 1896, a second lodge, known as the Gate City Rebekah Lodge, was created in Arkansas City as No. 309. These lodges consolidated on July 7, 1915. The Rebekah Lodge is the women's division of the IOOF. The first officers of the lodge were Mrs. Charles Leach, Noble Grand, and Anna Butler. The first meeting was held at the old Copple Building on East Central Avenue. Later, rooms were rented over the Bittle Building at Summit Street and Central Avenue. After the IOOF Hall was built, meetings were held there.

The Arkansas City Fortnightly Club was founded on February 23, 1892, in the home of Celia Foss Farrar. The Fortnightly Club was a literary and social club whose members strove for mutual improvement. One of the first projects that the group took on in Arkansas City was to collect books for a library. When a Carnegie library opened, the club donated more than 600 books.

63

The first record of the Commercial Club is dated to 1900 from a memory of Albert Newton. However, that is not when the club was organized. No one really knows for sure when it was started, but it was designed for businessmen to "promote the progress and prosperity of Arkansas City, cultivate harmonious public spirit and social quality among business men."

The Mother's Club was formed in 1912 in East Bolton Township by Mrs. T.B. Winslow, Mrs. G.I. Pike, and Mrs. Edwin Winslow. The members wanted to be involved in an organization that would help mothers be more closely associated with one another socially. They felt that it would make them more efficient parents, which would make for a better home life.

ROTARY CLUB 20 YEARS OLD

Local Organization Had Inception in 1914

The Rotary Club was founded in 1914. Rotary is an international organization based on service to one's profession and community as well as to the club. Initially, Rotarians promoted charity for boys and the handicapped. They encourage fellow members to participate in civic enterprises. The Rotary Club continues to do much good in the community today.

The Arkansas City Jaycees were organized in 1919. It was the second chapter anywhere. Local Jaycees worked on community projects throughout the years. One of their greatest accomplishments was when they organized the Cherokee Strip Land Rush Museum in 1966. Jaycees were also involved in starting the car racetrack and working with children with cerebral palsy. Up until 2005, the Ark City chapter was the longest-running chapter in the world, having not ever let its charter drop.

Lions Club Here Was Born In 1920; A Thriving Group

The Arkansas City Lions Club was organized on November 22, 1920, at a meeting at the Osage Hotel. The group is a nonpolitical, nonsectarian organization composed of business people (men at that time) who are interested in welfare and progress of the community. The first local president was Dr. C.H. House, the first vice president was Luther Parman, and the second vice president was Lloyd Lesh.

The Arkansas City Kiwanis Club was founded in March 1923. The group was established for businessmen and professionals who banded together for "mutual and general uplift." It stresses loyalty to the United States, promotes business ethics, and encourages civic betterment projects. Kiwanis members have always helped underprivileged children. Today, their projects remain dedicated to children.

Members of Petroleum Club Have Many Fine Features In Their Commodious Club House

The Arkansas City Petroleum Club was formed in 1926. It was set up for businessmen, professionals, and oilmen as a civic and pleasure club, meaning members helped others, but in their club room they had dances, a handball court, a radio set, and more. The club had lunchrooms and several suites with living rooms and bedrooms. This was to provide lodging for men on the road for business.

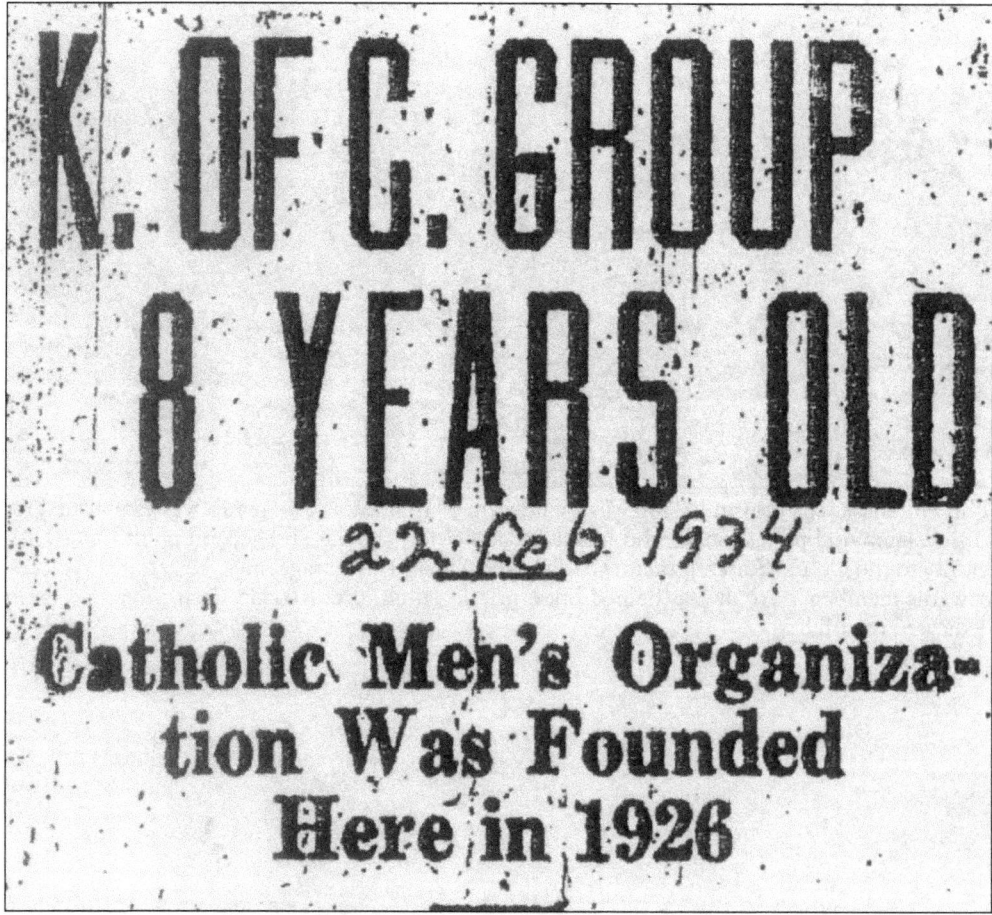

K. OF C. GROUP 8 YEARS OLD

22 Feb 1934

Catholic Men's Organization Was Founded Here in 1926

The Arkansas City Knights of Columbus, Council No. 2614, was organized in 1926. It is an organization for Catholic men. The principles behind the club are charity, unity, fraternity, and patriotism. The Knights of Columbus undertake many projects, but one of their main focuses today is to raise money for local mental health services and to help fund the Special Olympics.

Six

CHURCHES

As in most communities, one of the first things brought to Arkansas City when it was settled was religion. To many people, a community is not a town until there is a divine presence in it. Arkansas City was founded in 1870, and the first church began to be organized that same year.

By April 24, 1870, the first services were held by Rev. B.C. Swartz. He established the First Methodist Episcopal and served as its pastor for two years. Services were sometimes held in a tent and sometimes in the blacksmith shop on West Central Avenue. The pulpits and benches were built by George Walker and Ira Smith. By January 24, 1874, plans were made for a permanent building. The location was to be 107 South Second Street. Brick for the construction of the church was made at the Walnut River, south of Madison Avenue.

Another of the first houses of worship was a Methodist church. It started being used in 1875, before the tower was finished or the walls were plastered. The windows and benches were covered in muslin. The youth gave a temperance play in 1875 called "Ten Nights in a Bar Room." It was 1883 before the church was dedicated. By 1909, the congregation needed a new building, which was constructed at the corner of Fifth Avenue and Second Street. The cornerstone for the church was not laid until 1912, and its dedication was on April 6, 1913. The Young Ladies Aid Society purchased a bell for the tower.

As in many small communities, the church buildings were used for multiple purposes until other facilities could be built. On June 4, 1880, the first Arkansas City High School graduating class had its commencement at the First United Methodist Church. The structure was used for choir concerts, and the church bell sounded fire alarms.

Though the First Methodist Episcopal Church was the first church in Arkansas City, many followed. They were largely built by their congregations, and groups within the church body often raised money for expansions. Many of the early churches are still in use, and they are some of the most beautiful buildings in town.

The first church building in Arkansas City was known as the white church. It was erected in the summer and fall of 1873. It was known as the "liberal church" because it was for the use of any denomination. Mrs. Mowry, Margery Thompson, Dillie Collings, and Mrs. Sipes drove 12 miles all across the countryside to gather corn to sell in order to help raise funds for the church. When it came time to plaster, Mrs. W.M. Benedict and Mrs. Hay had a New England supper to pay for it.

The United Presbyterian Church was formed on January 16, 1873. Until the church was completed, the congregation met in Peter Pierson's Hall. All work was done by volunteers. The cottonwood lumber was milled at Sleeth's mill. Finishing lumber was hauled from Wichita. Thomas Baird supplied this lumber. All of the money for other supplies was raised by the congregation. The church continues to be in use.

The First Presbyterian Church was organized on January 12, 1873, by Rev. A.R. Naylor. The first meeting was in the office of Meigs and Walton, where the charter was formed. Meetings were held in a small building at 207 South Summit Street until a new church was built at 311 South First Street. The lots were given to the church by C.M. Scott.

The Pilgrim Congregational Church was organized in 1887 under the leadership of Rev. David DeLong. The congregation met in various places until the basement at Third Street and Central Avenue was built in 1891. Church members met there until a church building was completed in April 1893.

The Church of Christ, Scientist began to hold services in Arkansas City in 1888. Fanny E. Wilkins of Beatrice, Nebraska, was the reader. Services were held in the Houghton Building on Summit Street, then at the Fifth Avenue Opera House, then at Highland Hall. In 1900, the Christian Science meeting was moved to a remodeled residence on Second Street. In 1915, the current building was erected at the corner of A Street and Chestnut Avenue.

The first Catholic church in Arkansas City was built at the current location of Wilson Park. It was moved in 1889 to Fifth Avenue and A Street, where it became somewhat of a community landmark. Catholics and non-Catholics alike had a very soft spot for the Reverend Father Degnan, who tended his flock there. The present church was constructed in 1919 and dedicated in November 1920, after a lot of work from the congregation and Frank J. Hess, who sealed the deal for the land.

The First Baptist Church was founded in 1882 in a temporary location. The original church building was dedicated in 1885 at Central Avenue and A Street. In 1912, the congregation began efforts to construct a new church. The building was finally dedicated in 1928. It has been at B Street and Central Avenue ever since.

The first plans for the Trinity Episcopal Church were made in 1884. The church was actually founded in 1887, and a temporary place of worship was erected on the corner of Third Avenue and Fifth Street. The congregation had plans to erect a larger structure as membership grew. In 1920, the church purchased four lots and a house on the northeast corner of the 200 block of North A Street. The present building was completed in 1923 at a cost of $65,000.

Central Christian Church was established in 1877. Members began to meet by Parker Cemetery until the congregation grew so big that it moved to a hall at the present location of the Burford Theater. Churchgoers then met in the First Ward School building. The first church edifice was a 28-foot-by-30-foot building that cost $1,800. Today, the church is a large building that houses a full congregation.

Pilgrim Rest Church was first organized in 1888 with Mack Delaino as the minister. It was an African American church located at 517 North A Street. In 1944, plans were made to move the church, and 11 lots were purchased at 525 North Fifth Street. Designs were drawn up for the new church in 1945, but it was not completed and moved into until 1957.

The Salvation Army has been operating in Arkansas City since 1909. It moved around for a time but in 1939 built a citadel at 107 West Walnut Avenue. It was constructed during the command of Maj. Leon Geer and his wife. After some time, the Salvation Army outgrew this citadel and moved several times to larger buildings in Arkansas City.

Seven
LAW ENFORCEMENT

Arkansas City law enforcement has a long and colorful history. From the 1890s—when the police hauled prostitutes into the courtroom to pay their monthly fines so they would not have to be picked up for another month—to the Prohibition era—when the police mounted machine guns to airplane wings—Arkansas City's officers have had busy and interesting jobs.

In the 1880s, police mainly handled horse and cattle thefts, robberies, and prostitution. They pursued Jesse James across the county after he robbed the Cowley County Bank and chased out other outlaws who tried to make Arkansas City the site of their next heist.

In 1893, there was a rash of horses stolen from those seeking to stake claims in the Cherokee Strip Land Rush. Ora Deakon, from Trinidad, Colorado, had his horse stolen. A gentleman from Larned, Kansas, reported his horse stolen from in front of Hess Real Estate where it was hitched. The Larned man went on the trail to an area 23 miles from Trinidad, Colorado, and found the horses and the thief. He wired back to Arkansas City that he had found them, and Marshal Rarick sent orders back to have the thieves arrested. He sent Officer Gray to pick them up and bring them back to Arkansas City.

Hunting outlaws was not the only duty to befall police officers in Arkansas City. In 1905, City Councilman Smith had made so many outrageous suggestions that the local newspaper suggested the city commission add the following: putting up clothes lines throughout the district, caring for babies whose mothers want to go calling, settling neighborhood and family quarrels, milking cows, cutting grass in lawns, arguing politics, explaining city ordinances, catching peddlers who are operating without a license, regulating clocks, seeing that butcher boys and grocery deliverymen did not chin the cooks, stopping fast-driving vehicles, establishing grades, assisting in making street improvements, instructing the engineer at the waterworks in the proper way to sound the fire alarm, building smokes to prevent mosquitoes, and keeping diary of daily happenings. The police of the day were certainly involved in a bit of everything.

In later times, police officers in Arkansas City dealt with crashing stills and raiding many joints during Prohibition, which was a difficult time for law enforcement. There are stories of officers raiding houses and pubs and taking huge supplies of liquor from them. Sometimes, officers had to chain up illegal gambling devices. Police even chased robbers from the air by mounting machine guns to airplanes' wings and following the culprits until they were caught. It has been a tradition that an Arkansas City policeman be resilient and stay on the trail of a criminal until he or she is caught.

One of these officers is believed to be Capt. Orin Sumner (O.S.) Rarick. Rarick was born in Ohio in 1839. He was in the Civil War and afterward served under General Barrett in Indian Territory, where he became a US marshal. Later, Rarick came to Arkansas City where he was a constable, city marshal, deputy sheriff, and sheriff. He served on the force for 15 years.

W.J. "Uncle Billy" Gray was an Arkansas City police officer from 1872 to 1925. He served as a constable afterward until 1929. During all the years that he was on the force, Gray never shot a man. At 70 years old, he was still serving as a constable. (Courtesy of Randy Walker.)

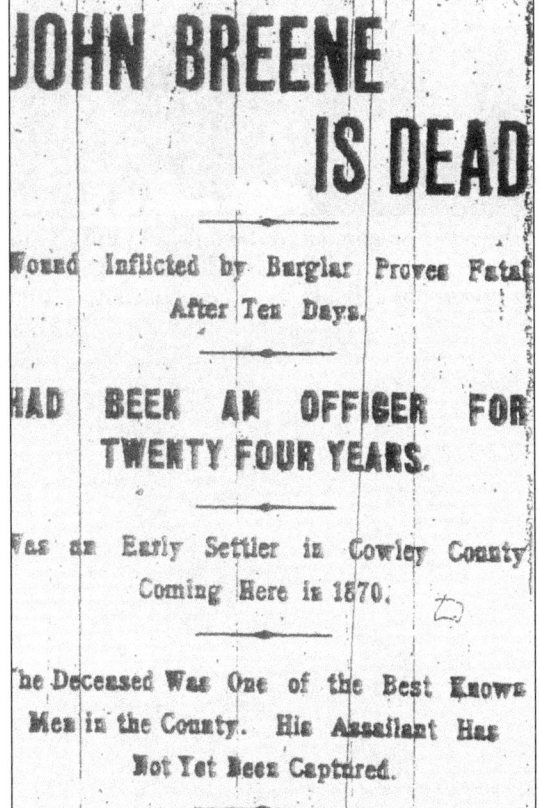

JOHN BREENE IS DEAD

Wound Inflicted by Burglar Proves Fatal After Ten Days.

HAD BEEN AN OFFICER FOR TWENTY FOUR YEARS.

Was an Early Settler in Cowley County Coming Here in 1870.

The Deceased Was One of the Best Known Men in the County. His Assailant Has Not Yet Been Captured.

John Breene came to Arkansas City in 1870. He lived on a claim in Geuda Springs for a while but sold it and came to Arkansas City. Breene clerked at a few stores and later became a constable. When George H. McIntire was elected sheriff, Breene was his deputy. In 1888, he became a constable again due to McIntire's term expiring. Breene was constable and sheriff for 24 years. In 1906, he awoke to an intruder, and a gunfight ensued. He was shot and later died from the wound.

83

In September 1905, officers took Ole Jim and the police wagon out to the railroad yards to run off a hobo. The man would not get out of the yards, so Marshal Callahan loaded up the hobo and took him to jail. Ole Jim was once the fire wagon horse, but he became a police horse and went out on calls with the officers.

George W. Simms was the city marshal and chief of police from 1907 to 1909. He kept the peace in town until he was practically beaten to death by the Cornish brothers near the Pastime Theater.

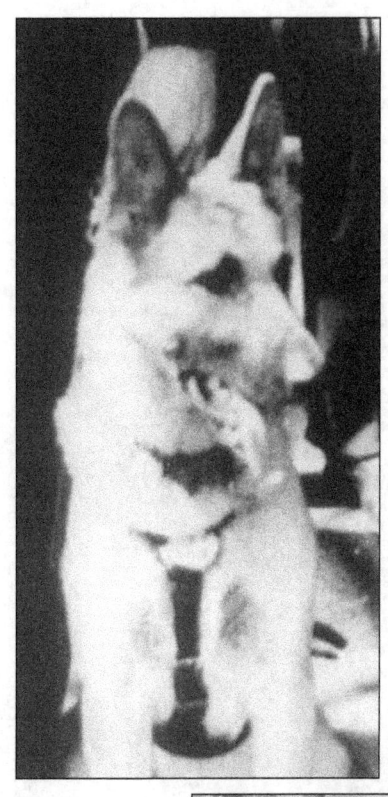

In Arkansas City, as with other towns, police dogs have been used through the years. Several of the dogs in Arkansas City became very well known. Dogs of note include Duke, Dock, Grover, and Brownie. Grover originally belonged to Elwin Hunt, but he formed a liking to officer J.E. Nash. Once Nash left the department, the dog stayed and continued to make the rounds. He died on February 1, 1905. Brownie was a brown and white bird dog who belonged to Capt. Clay Lemert, a former National Guard commander. When his owner was reassigned, Brownie followed officer Herman Pratt on rounds and was fed by local restaurants. In 1947, his owner came back, and Brownie retired from the force. (Both courtesy of Randy Walker.)

May 1963

1st	Row	Gerald Fry with Duke, Julius Pack, Merton Darnall, Sam Brown, Amos Barton with Dock.
2nd	Row	Paul Lesh, Marvin Hatfield, Milton Jordan, Hugh Killblane, Bill Bowker, Harold Peterson, Hazel Moore, Jim Lowery.
3rd	Row	Frank Robertson, Vic Franklin, Herman Fisher, Jack Fortenberry, Don Wahlemaier, Bill Rice.

Police chief Floyd Higgins had light signals installed on the Highland Hotel and Newman's Building in 1924 that would alert the police if they needed to call into the station. Up to this point, officers walking their beat had to call in every 15 minutes. Afterward, they would look for the lights to know whether to call in or not.

POLICE CHIEF ADVOCATES NEW SIGNAL SYSTEM

Licensing Of Hotels And Rooming Houses Also Recommended.

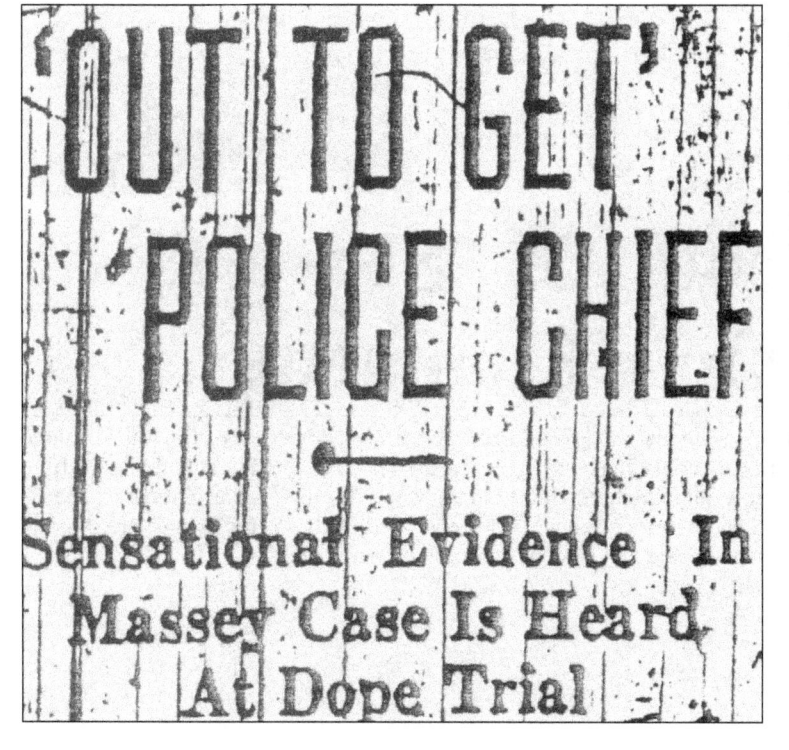

'OUT TO GET' POLICE CHIEF

Sensational Evidence In Massey Case Is Heard At Dope Trial

On July 29, 1925, there was a court case in which Henry "Red" Massey was arrested and charged with selling and possessing morphine. Charles Lee was the arresting officer. Massey's case was based upon the claim that Lee framed him because Massey had a vendetta against Chief Higgins, who had fired him twice. Lee had actually taken his wife to Massey's home to make a purchase. There was conflict in the testimony, and the jury failed to come to a consensus.

AX DROPS ON MATRON AND TWO OFFICERS

Dismissals Are For "Good Of Service" Only Comment

On May 2, 1925, Chief Floyd Higgins was given instructions by Mayor Boggs that he was in charge of the police department and could make whatever decisions he chose. Higgins released three employees—Charles Lee, William Lemmon, and Emma Ray. The chief had attempted to do this before but had been blocked by former mayors. It is believed that these employees were directly linked to the morphine bust of Red Massey. New employees were hired.

In 1933, city manager Clyde King allowed police chief Clint Robinson to purchase a Thompson submachine gun for the department. The gun was used for several incidents in town. One such instance was when the sheriff took the "tommy gun" to the Missouri Pacific train yards and fired it into an old wash boiler. He was attempting to scare a group of hobos away because he suspected they were responsible for a robbery. The gun decimated the boiler, so the hobos hightailed it out of there. The next day, the group was back, so Robinson switched the gun to semiautomatic and fired into more boilers. He looked at the hobos and told them that if he came back tomorrow he might be "a little more nervous with the gun."

Lester Richardson joined the Arkansas City Police Department in 1926 as a night patrolman. In 1934, he was made chief. During his tenure, he worked hard to rid the town of marijuana. He tendered his resignation in 1945.

Hugh Killblane was a police officer with the Arkansas City Police Department a total of 14 years and was a deputy sheriff for Cowley County for 11. He was a motorcycle police officer as well and made several trips to and from Winfield at more than 100 miles per hour while carrying blood for the hospital. In November 1938, Killblane was riding with Tom Goodson when a call came over the radio that Pretty Boy Floyd was at the Chevy garage. The officers took off in that direction. Before they got there, Goodson made a wrong turn. Killblane said, "I think you made a wrong turn." Goodson's reply was, "No, I didn't. We'll live longer if we go this way!"

Arkansas City got its first motorcycle police officer on July 21, 1931: Charles Noble. The City of Arkansas City purchased an Indian motorcycle, and Noble paid the city for it each month. When his service was over, he kept the bike. Ed Hamilton was the motorcycle police officer in January 1938. His bike was a Harley-Davidson. On November 28, 1938, Hugh Killblane (above) took over the job.

On January 15, 1945, Walter Gray, former night police captain, was appointed chief of police by city manager Clyde B. King. Gray was the successor to Lester Richardson. In Gray's first year as chief, drunkenness was the leading cause for arrests. During his tenure, he broke a burglary ring that had been rampant in the community. The police questioned George A. Haier (alias Brown) for three days in order to break the ring. The other two suspects, Garfield E. Allen and Wordie Cunningham, both of Wichita, confessed easily once they heard Brown had talked. Gray was also responsible for busting up clubs where underage drinkers were being admitted.

Clifford Smiley worked for the Arkansas City Police Department for 30 years. He started with the department in 1926 and by the time he retired had worked under seven chiefs of police. Smiley worked for 10 years on night duty and was then given a daytime desk job. When he worked nights, he was a foot policeman. He said that patrolmen worked in pairs: one pair walked the alleys of Summit Street, while another pair walked Summit Street itself. Smiley remembered that there were not any traffic problems when he was a rookie, but he did spend lots of time chasing bootleggers. Smiley retired in 1956 at the age of 69. (Both courtesy of Randy Walker.)

Eight
HOSPITALS

Arkansas City has had a long history of health care. There have been several hospitals, a nurses' training school, a few clinics, and many doctors. Before the hospitals came along, doctors served their patients from their homes.

Early on, there were three hospitals in town at one time: Mercy Hospital, A.C. Hospital, and Stricklen Hospital. In 1930, all three together could serve 141 patients. Each of the hospitals strove to be cutting-edge and offered top-notch care for its visitors.

The hospitals of Arkansas City grew along with the community. As the town became more settled and population increased, the medical centers had to accommodate more patients. Even though there were three hospitals, they still dealt with overcrowding. Therefore, as years passed by, the hospitals had to expand several times and even rebuild.

Today, Arkansas City is still facing issues with failing buildings and old equipment. In 2010, construction began on a new hospital that promises to be a state-of-the-art facility. Both the hospital and the community hope that the new medical center will bring in specialists from around the country to serve Arkansas City and the surrounding area.

The Mercy Hospital was built in 1905. Located at 801 North First Street, it was remodeled in 1925. By 1930, its value was $80,000. The hospital was an incorporated business with several of the doctors as stockholders. It had 50 private rooms and two wards: one for men and one for women. Each ward had three beds. The doctors who were on staff in 1930 were L.M. Beatson, A.J. Berger, E.H. Clayton, J.H. Douglas, B.C. Geeslin, E.F. Day, E.W. Helweg, H.A. Mercer, B.A. Spaulding, E.A. Tufts, W.H. Ray, C.R. Spain, W.F. Zugg, and C.A. Wilson, DDS.

A.C. Hospital opened on July 4, 1906. It was owned by Dr. R.L. Ferguson and Dr. R.C. Young and was located at 828 South B Street. The institution had 30 rooms, four operating rooms, an X-ray room, a laboratory, and elevators. A.C. Hospital was said to have been a very modern facility.

During the preparations for A.C. Hospital, Doctor Young and Doctor Payne planned for an attic in which the nurses could live.

The Arkansas City Hospital

828 South B Street
Martha Philips, Matron

The first hospital ever operated in Arkansas City.

This hospital is equipped with a corps of the best trained nurses in the state of Kansas.

For service and equipment this hospital is unexcelled.

Conducted on most ethical basis. All recognized physicians welcome. Trained nurses furnished at your home on application.

In 1907, the hospital had grown so much that Doctor Young and Doctor Day contemplated shutting the hospital down so they could add on to the original structure. This proposal did not work, however, because there were still patients who needed care. As a result, patients stayed in the hospital while the renovations occurred. After construction was completed, the hospital was one of the most sufficient in the region. There were an additional 12 rooms, giving the hospital a total of 28 with the capacity for 32 beds. The equipment was modern. A kitchen and dining room were on the first floor, and the private rooms and ward were on the second floor. The hospital's doctors invited members of all of the town's churches to bring flowers to the patients, and all doctors in the community were welcomed to use the facility.

The nurses' training school was incorporated into the A.C. Hospital in 1907. Women who enrolled attended courses for three years. Mrs. J.B. O'Connor was put in charge of the girls on September 3, 1928.

WILL BUILD NEW HOSPITAL.

Thirty-five Room Modern Structure Made of White Brick.

Plans are in Hands of Local Contractors at Present.—Work to Begin in Very Near Future.

In 1913, Doctor Young and Doctor Brock decided to build a new hospital on South B Street. It was to be built where the hospital was at the time. The medical facility had grown to the point that it again needed more room due to a fire that partially destroyed the hospital. There were to be wider corridors, a larger room for the nurses' training school, and more rooms for patients. Construction of the new hospital began in May and finished in July. In 1917, it was expanded again to include new operating rooms, a lecture hall, and more patient rooms.

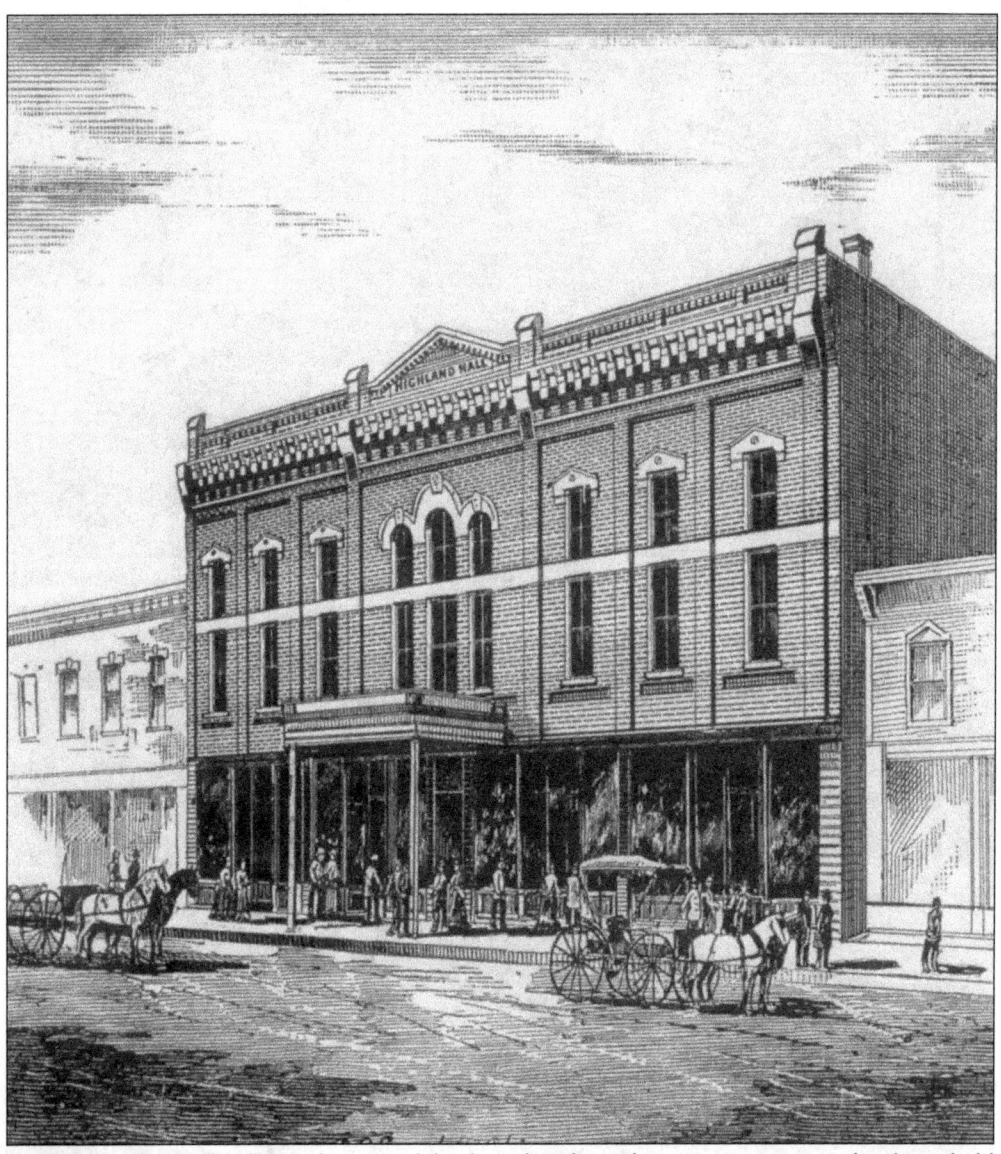

On October 20, 1908, the graduation of the first class from the nurses' training school was held at Highland Hall. The ceremony opened with MacAlister's Orchestra, a prayer was offered by the Rev. George O. Nichols of the First Presbyterian Church, and the addresses were made by Doctor Bradford, dean of Epworth University at Oklahoma City, and Dr. R.C. Young. Music was provided by Katherine Strack, of Winfield, and then the procession occurred.

In 1917, the hospital closed temporarily because the owners, Doctor Young and Doctor Brock, went into service during World War I. On February 1, 1919, it reopened and remained in service to the community until May 14, 1946, when Young closed the facility. It was later used for apartments. On August 22, 1928, the Stricklen Hospital opened at 1227–1231 North First Street. It was owned by Dr. H.M. Stricklen, the head surgeon. There were 27 private rooms and one ward with five beds. The hospital had portable X-ray machines, oxygen bottles, and an incubator. It also had a baby room with bassinets. There was an ambulance drive on the right side of the hospital. The building was heated by steam and was decorated with beautiful walnut furniture from the Brown and Miller store. The hospital stayed in operation until 1946, when Stricklen died in his sleep after a heart attack.

In 1944, the City of Arkansas City began to map out a municipal hospital. The chamber of commerce proposed a bill in the Kansas Legislature that the hospital would be a memorial to the men and women in the armed forces. The law would allow the city commission to authorize bonds up to $350,000 for purchasing a site and erecting the hospital as well as a nurses' training school on-site. It would also allow the local government to have full control over the money in the fund. By 1945, the city had chosen architects William T. Schmitt and W.G. Parr from Oklahoma City to design the hospital. A site was chosen north of Wilson Park between Summit and First Streets. The plans were detailed as follows: a three-story concrete structure with 12 single-bed rooms, around 60 beds total, a basement, two operating rooms, obstetrical rooms, a nursery, pharmacy, emergency treatment room, laundry room, and an isolation ward.

In October 1949, a contract was let to Marshall-Kerr Construction, of Tulsa, for the construction of the hospital. The new medical facility was opened to the public the second Sunday of March 1951. After the open house, a few days were taken to add finishing touches, and the hospital was open for business.

The Only Incorporated Hospital in The City

---Mercy Hospital---

Successor to

The Arkansas City Hospital.

801 North First St., Arkansas City, Kans.

Address all communication to Laura Bull, Matron.

DIRECTORS	
E. Kirkpatrick, Pres.	Built and controlled by the business men of Arkansas City, and open to all reputable physicians.
P. E. Henneberry, Vice Pres.	
A. J. Hunt, Sec.	
A. H. Denton, Treas.	
C. M. Scott	Rooms furnished by the different churches, lodges and charitable organizations of the city. One of the few hospitals of the state receiving a state appropriation.
H. P. Farrar	
W. E. Wilcox	
C. H. Searing	
Chas. Williams	
O. E. Unsell	
C. N. Hunt	
J. H. Hamilton	
N. D. Sanders	
Earl Newman	Nurses training school in connection with hospital. Nurses supplied on application.
C. T. Wells	
Thos. Baird	
Geo. D. Ormiston	

The old Mercy Hospital was renovated and used as a unit of the Arkansas City Memorial Hospital. The building provided extra rooms and isolation wards. This left the facility with 64 beds, 20 bassinets, and two cribs in the new building, as well as 29 beds in the old building.

Nine
SCHOOLS

Arkansas City has a long and successful history of education. From its inception, the city has had a school. The first was in the home of Prof. H.B. Norton, brother to Capt. H.G. Norton, who was the leader of the group that founded Arkansas City. H.B.'s home was at the northwest corner of Birch Avenue and A Street. The first teacher in Arkansas City was Mary Elizabeth "Lizzy" Swarts.

In 1872, the first common schools were developed in Arkansas City as a result of the county school system. The first public school in town was a wooden building at 205 South Summit Street. This school was moved a few times, and over time more schools were added. Through the years, the schools have changed both locations and names, but the quality of education has always been excellent.

One of the interesting things about Arkansas City is that it has never had segregated schools. All children attended the same classes. That is not to say that there were never race issues, but it is refreshing that the people of Arkansas City were far-sighted enough to recognize that every child should be able to have the same level of education. There were racial issues among individuals and sometimes there were conflicts involving extracurricular activities, but that was not the norm. Members of the African American community who attended the schools have differing opinions on the treatment of minorities.

In general, most students who attended Arkansas City schools felt a strong bond with their alma mater. Many share fond memories of the schools, their experiences there, and their teachers.

In 1874, the common school was moved to a brick building called First Ward in the 300 block of North B Street. In 1872, E.H. Hulse was hired as a superintendent and a principal was hired for the school. Also in 1874, two elementary teachers were hired. Hulse taught the high school classes. The school ran under the supervision of the county between 1872 and 1888. The first high school class of five students graduated in 1880. In 1888, the school was enlarged and became solely an elementary school. First Ward School later became known as Roosevelt Elementary School.

Strangely enough, the Fourth Ward Elementary School, also known as Central School, was organized in 1885, before the Second Ward or Third Ward Schools. In 1924, the building underwent a two-room addition. W.H. Underhill of Wichita, Kansas, was the company that did the renovations. The 40 men constantly working on the job had heating and plumbing installed that summer. Instead of expanding the walls, two 14-foot wings were added on the north side of the building. There were also extra windows put into the existing structure to make the lighting better. The school was later named Frances Willard Elementary.

Later known as Lincoln School, Second Ward Elementary School was built in Arkansas City in 1886. The building was brick and limestone. In 1920, it began a kindergarten program, and in 1921, the PTA was organized. There were 103 members and at least 80 attended each meeting. They purchased books and playground equipment for the school.

Third Ward Elementary School was built in 1887. It was on an original hunting ground south of the canal at Sixth Street and Madison Avenue. The structure was brick and limestone. Furniture was purchased from Grand Rapids School and Furniture Company of Grand Rapids, Michigan. It was of the most modern style and was especially nice. The building had steam heating and the latest in comfort. Due to flooding issues, the school was moved to the 1100 block of South Third Street and was later renamed Washington Elementary School.

From 1888 to 1891, a house at 115 South First Street was rented from H.P. Farrar to be used as the high school. It had once been a boardinghouse and was located in a grove of trees. Many referred to the school as "forest house." However, when bed bugs were found in the cracks and crevices of the building, the school was unofficially dubbed "Bed Bug Hall."

In 1889, the superintendent of the high school, David Boyd, hired Charles Sedgwick, a noted architect from Minneapolis, Minnesota, to design a new high school building. The school board sold bonds in the amount of $49,000 in order to construct the school. The architect alone cost the board $19,000. Work began on the school on July 10, 1890. The building was to be constructed with limestone and vermillion pigment in the mortar. However, the pigment was not waterproofed and the dye cast a red hue on the school the first time it rained.

The high school building was actually erected by local stone and marble masons Joseph Bossi, Antonio Buzzi, and Charles Fredrick Rothfus. M.E. Roderick carved the snarling lions at the main entrance on Central Avenue. When the school was completed, it was a sight to behold. The first floor had a fountain in the center of the entrance hall with plants around it. The superintendent's office and the boardroom were covered in Brussels carpet and had fireplaces. At the time the school opened in 1893, L.E. Eddy was principal, and there were two other teachers on staff, Martin Reid and Adah Vivion.

High school sports did not exist in Arkansas City until 1905. The first team organized in the Arkansas City school system was a girls' basketball team formed by Roxanna Oldroyd, the chemistry and physics instructor, who wanted an activity for girls.

Boys' basketball started in 1906. The founder is unknown, but by 1908, Francis Schmidt was the coach for both the boys' and girls' teams. Eventually, the schools incorporated other sports for which the Arkansas City school system has become quite well known.

In 1910, the board of education authorized the construction of a manual training school at 200 South Third Street. The three-level brick building was designed by Thomas Williamson and Company of Topeka, Kansas. The school had four pillars on the west side and a new, up-to-date air circulating system. It was a vocational school, but art and music were taught there as well. The manual training school underwent remodeling in 1917.

The junior high program started in America in the early 20th century. It usually included grades seven through nine. In Arkansas City, the board of education built a school south of the manual training school to accommodate the program. The junior high school was completed in the spring of 1918. It cost the school system $100,000. The building contained an auditorium, a gymnasium, a library, laboratories, offices, and 16 classrooms. The junior high school, which then included the manual training school, was dedicated on May 16, 1918.

115

In 1921, Edna L. Johnson, a teacher, presented an English bulldog to the football team. The dog was supposed to be named Anthony, but he was not formerly introduced. It was not until 1950 that a bulldog logo was designed. Linda Linnenkohl created it and painted it on the sidewalk in front of school. The name Sally was given to the dog at some point, and it has been thus ever since.

In 1922, a new senior high school was built in the 200 block of South Second Street. It was located to the east of the junior high. The building was also designed by Thomas Williamson and Company of Topeka, Kansas. Contractor George Gassman constructed the three-level building of brick and limestone. The 87,547-square-foot school cost $250,000. The building had both circulating heat and air conditioning. Its entrance had two English Gothic towers. The senior high school was connected to the junior high by two passageways, one on the north and one on the south.

In 1935, the city submitted an application to the Public Works Administration board for construction of a place for people to gather. Once approved, the project became a joint effort between the city and the school district. The city moved to create a field house similar to the Washburn University Field House. The architect, Tom Williamson, worked toward that line. The 170-foot-by-140-foot building was erected at the northeast corner of Fifth Avenue and Second Street on the property that was formerly owned by Mrs. C.M. Scott and John Probst. It seated 4,000 people. The first major event held there was the ninth Coronation of Queen Alalah in the fall of 1936.

In 1982, yet another high school came into being. The current school was in need of massive repairs too extensive for the school district to justify. A new building was constructed on West Radio Lane on land purchased from Cowley College. The cost of this school was $10,200,000. It opened January 3, 1983.

Ten

CHILOCCO INDIAN AGRICULTURAL SCHOOL

Because it was only three miles from town, the Chilocco Indian Agricultural School in Oklahoma has occupied a significant part of Arkansas City's history. Chilocco was a school set up by the US government to "Americanize" Native American tribes. On May 17, 1882, Congress authorized the construction of the school. It was not until 1885, however, that it was officially opened.

The campus for Chilocco originally occupied 1,119.06 acres of land and was increased to 8,640 acres when the Cherokee Tribe deeded some of its land over to the school. Chilocco was first known as Haworth Institute, named for the first superintendent of the school, Maj. James M. Haworth of Olathe, Kansas. Its name was later changed to Chilocco Indian Industrial School and later still to Chilocco Indian Agricultural School.

The focus of the school was agriculture. The children were also taught several skills that would help them integrate into a white world. They learned how to handle money, job skills, and other household chores.

The stories of Chilocco are not always positive. In the beginning, children were taken from their parents and their tribes and forced to attend the school. They were not allowed to speak their own languages or practice any of their customs. Children were not allowed to go home until after graduation. This was an attempt by the federal government to finally rid the country of conflicts with Native Americans. Instead of fighting more battles, the plan was to raise the children to behave "properly" in a white society.

Though this was the initial reason for the boarding school, over time the purpose for the school changed to a more positive experience, where the kids who attended were not just there to learn white ways. They experienced camaraderie with one another and shared in many of the same experiences as other schools. They organized clubs and organizations as well as played sports.

Chilocco staff and students spent a lot of time on Arkansas City on shopping excursions, attending festivities, and playing sports. In turn, many people visited the campus for sporting events and to attend cultural activities such as powwows. The citizens of Arkansas City developed a great relationship with the school and the people there. Not only is there a remaining sense of affection for the school by its former teachers, staff, and students, but there also remains a nostalgic feeling toward the school by people of Arkansas City who spent time there.

Chilocco was originally a small campus. In 1905, when this photograph was taken, there were still very few buildings.

In later years, the Chilocco campus was quite extensive. There were buildings for classes and activities as well as dorms. The property contained a store, a café, a swimming pool, fields for sporting events, and other facilities. It had its own water tower and a cemetery for many of the children who passed away while at the school.

By 1904, boys spent their time farming and often ran their own farm. They were allowed to keep one-fourth of the profits from crops. Students both grew produce and raised farm animals, which they learned to care for and showed at fairs and such.

121

The girls were taught to keep house. They worked in mock homes, cooking, cleaning, and sewing. They often made their own clothes and curtains for their rooms. They also worked in the school's kitchen and in the bakery.

The children learned trades and home skills, and they also attended classes in math, science, geography, history, and many other core subjects.

There were also skills learned that are not traditionally taught in schools or used often around the home. Some girls learned to weave, and boys learned leatherwork, boot repair, and similar crafts.

The Chilocco students participated in extracurricular activities just as students at any other school would have. Many of the pupils played in the band, which held concerts and marched in parades, such as Arkalalah, along with Chilocco dancers.

Not only did students play in band, but they also were able to perform in theater productions on campus such as the *First Thanksgiving* and the *Birth of Christ*. The plays were very Eurocentric in nature.

125

Chilocco was well known for its athletic programs. In the region, many schools competed with Chilocco in football, baseball, basketball, wrestling, and boxing. The school was best known for its boxers. There were several state and national champions on the Chilocco team.

Chilocco's football team was highly competitive. Many people in the Arkansas City area remember playing football against Chilocco. The players were known for speed and agility.

www.arcadiapublishing.com

Discover books about the town where you grew up, the cities where your friends and families live, the town where your parents met, or even that retirement spot you've been dreaming about. Our Web site provides history lovers with exclusive deals, advanced notification about new titles, e-mail alerts of author events, and much more.

MADE IN THE USA

Arcadia Publishing, the leading local history publisher in the United States, is committed to making history accessible and meaningful through publishing books that celebrate and preserve the heritage of America's people and places. Consistent with our mission to preserve history on a local level, this book was printed in South Carolina on American-made paper and manufactured entirely in the United States.

This book carries the accredited Forest Stewardship Council (FSC) label and is printed on 100 percent FSC-certified paper. Products carrying the FSC label are independently certified to assure consumers that they come from forests that are managed to meet the social, economic, and ecological needs of present and future generations.

FSC
Mixed Sources
Product group from well-managed forests and other controlled sources
Cert no. SW-COC-001530
www.fsc.org
© 1996 Forest Stewardship Council

Find Your Place in History.